Journey of Faith

Our Story

Journey of Faith

Our Story

BY DON JENKS

Journey of Faith
Our Story
by Don Jenks
Printed in the United States of America

1st Edition
ISBN: 979-8-234-07257-3

JOURNEY OF FAITH
OUR STORY

CONTENTS

Dedication

This book is dedicated to our precious family: 0ur three children - Julie and her husband, Jim; JoEllen; and our son, Jimmy. Our grandchildren: Josh; Nick and his wife, Sara; and Samantha. We also dedicate this book to our pastors and to our church family who have been there for us through both the good and difficult times. Many thanks to each one who brought us laughter, joy, and strength down throughout the years.

We also wish to thank Pastor Pam Bolton for her labor of love in making this book possible!

Lastly, we dedicate this book, *Journey of Faith Our Story,* to each one of you who are about to read it. My wife and I pray that you will discover just how personal God really is through a relationship with the Lord Jesus Christ and how long, wide, deep, and high is His love for you. He has a great plan for your life!

FOREWORD

Come! Travel with Don on his journey with Jesus. I'm confident you will see yourself along the way. Join with Patty as together they face life's challenges along the way. "They make beautiful music together," is both figurative and literal. They are indeed a "Dynamic Duo"! Don, who plays his guitar "upside down." Patty, whose sweet voice gives no trace of prior pain. Their faith is always "upbeat." You will easily recognize how their faith is their strength and stability in life's adversities. Your own faith will be enriched and encouraged by their faith!

Barb and I have known Don and Patty for over half a century. We can't really do justice in describing the infectious joy and consistency of the "overcoming faith" they have lived. We trust, however, that you will garner a portion of that joy and faith as you read their story. Only God knows, but this brief book may be sent to you for a specific purpose in your life. Ultimately, they just want to lift Jesus higher so that others may see Him better! Enjoy the Journey!

Reverend Wayne Hampton

Introduction

You've got to be kidding me! I thought as I gazed at the clock on my nightstand. The glowing red numbers proclaimed that it was 4:27 AM, and I was wide awake. *Seems like that's been happening a lot lately... waking up when it is still dark outside*. On this particular morning, I was reflecting on the journey of my life... precious memories of days gone by. Memories are like footprints in the sand that prove that you have lived, loved, and endured.

I remembered my childhood, growing up in the fifties and sixties... a time when life seemed so much simpler. In fact, it came in threes: *My Three Sons*; *The Three Stooges*; Peter, Paul, and Mary; The Kingston Trio; 3 Musketeer candy bars (you could break them in three parts and share with your friends); three channels on TV; three-speed bikes; etc. etc. etc.

I remembered meeting the love of my life, Patty Stevens, on a blind date and how we set out to establish a home and family. So much to remember... the births of each of our precious kids and the joy of watching them grow up.

Then my thoughts shifted to the most awesome event of our lives, when both Patty and I discovered that the God of the universe is up close and personal through His Son, The Lord Jesus Christ.

After becoming Christians, we soon discovered just how wide and deep the love of God is for us and all mankind, and we set out on a Great Adventure. The purpose of this little book is to show you that the God of the universe is for real and that He loves you very much!

Maybe you have made some bad choices in your life and don't think that there is any hope for you. Please know that Jesus is ready, willing, and able to forgive you and transform your life. He can give you a brand-new start if you will let Him. Just keep your heart wide open as you read the pages of this little book. Jesus has told us in the Bible, “Behold, I stand at the door and knock. If anyone hears My voice and opens the door, I will come in to him and dine with him, and he with Me.” Revelation 3:20

CHAPTER 1

THE EARLY DAYS

Each one of us is on a journey. For some, the journey is long; and for others, it is relatively short. There are those who find the journey to be reasonably easy and others who have endured a bumpy ride. One thing is for certain: From the cradle to the grave, each one of us must take the journey; and how we end up has a lot to do with our choices. There was a point in time when my journey led me to a place where I found faith in Jesus Christ. From then on, my life became a JOURNEY OF FAITH.

I grew up in the tiny hamlet of Kingsbury, New York that is situated in the Adirondack Mountains on Route 4, a main truck route to Vermont. I was born into a loving and secure family, and I have many wonderful memories of growing up in the fifties and sixties.

I remember pulling my wagon to the Kingsbury General Store to pick up an order of groceries for our family. The store was filled with all kinds of goodies including ice cream bars, nickel candy bars, fireballs, root beer barrels, soda for a dime, and just about anything else you can imagine. You also could buy a baseball, a pair of boots, and even an alarm clock.

Mrs. Sterns, the owner, was just about my height, 4'10," when I first started going to the store. I did manage to grow another foot over the years. Maybe I'll be back to Mrs. Sterns' height before it's over, due to the aging process.

Then there were the adventures with my little brother, David, and my best friend, George. Camping out under the stars… building a tree house complete with a triple bunk bed… swimming in Halfway Brook… just to mention a few. I especially enjoyed playing baseball, even though there were just four of us, three boys and a dog. Enough for a pitcher… a catcher… a batter… and Trixie, the German Shepherd, who took care of all fielding. She was amazing. Trixie could catch a line drive hardball but not without sustaining minor damage to her teeth. She also could find the home run balls that disappeared into the summer foliage. The problem was she never liked giving the ball back, so we would bribe her with a pail of water. Invariably, the ball would end up in the water!

Once, I even tried to fly. I made a wing out of lath wood and heavy plastic. Fortunately for me, I decided to abort my plan to jump from the second-story window of my friend's barn. In a burst of speed, my solo flight went off a hay wagon instead. Wilbur and Orville had nothing to fear from my endeavor. Man, did that ever hurt!

My JOURNEY OF FAITH actually began when I attended the Kingbury Baptist Church. My friend George's mom was a Christian, and she would make a deal with me. I could camp out with George if I would go to church with them that Sunday. It seemed like a fair deal, and in fact, I found that I liked church. In Sunday School Class, I began to learn about a man named Jesus, who loved people, went around doing good for everyone, and then willingly died on a cross to take the punishment that people deserved because of sin, so they could go to Heaven someday. Years later, when I'd be coming home from a bar, feeling alone and empty, I would pray to the One I had heard so much about in church.

In the summer of 1970, I had my first encounter with a Christian at my workplace. I was working as a ride operator at Gaslight Village Amusement Park in Lake George, and it soon became apparent that there was something very different about the fella I was working with. He didn't swear like I did when things went wrong. He was friendly, patient, and courteous; and he didn't have to work at it. It was genuine. He told me he was a Christian and that was evident. I found myself apologizing for my behavior and biting my lip to hold back my colorful language. This experience got me thinking there was something to this "Christianity." I can also remember watching Billy Graham on TV, and with tears streaming down my face, I realized I needed God, but I wasn't quite ready to make that decision for myself.

CHAPTER 2

POP

"Donald, did you break the fence?!" Pop, my dad, had been looking out the window of the Ray Jenks Garage and spotted his four-year-old son jumping up and down on the fence out front. The poor old fence had finally given way under the enthusiastic assault of my forty-three pound frame.

"No, Dad, I didn't break the fence." Now this was a very wrong answer as I was about to learn!

"Donald, I saw you break the fence, and now I'm going to spank you, not because you broke the fence but because you lied to me." I think Pop must have understood the unbridled energy of a four-year-old boy. Dad swiftly administered justice and taught me a lesson that I would never forget. I purposed in my heart to never do that again.

Well, it was approximately fifteen years later when I didn't exactly do it again. I did omit some important facts about the matter at hand.

I had finished playing ball with some friends down the road and was jumping into my 1963 Ford Galaxy (it had a 351 under the hood). My buddies were egging me on to see how fast I could go. The engine roared to life, literally one glass pack muffler and a straight pipe exhaust system. I proceeded to jam the gas pedal to the floor and was racing down the road. The shift from first to second gear went fine; however, second to third presented a problem. The cheap shifter jammed between the two gears, and the transmission locked up, causing my poor car to shudder to a horrific demise just a few feet from my dad's garage!

Now, I'm sure that Pop must have heard the ruckus outside… a thunderous roar… squealing tires… followed by sudden silence! "Uh, Dad," I sheepishly said when entering the garage, "something happened to my transmission." I braced myself for His reaction. To my complete amazement, Pop never said a word about the incident and set out to fix my car! He must have been laughing on the inside.

I always had a tremendous respect for my father. He taught me to be honest, work hard, and to never give up. I never saw anyone work as hard as Pop. I remember him coming home from Monahan and Loughlan Steel Fabrication Shop, eating dinner, and then going out to the garage where he would be painting cars, building machines, or fixing radiators until one o'clock in the morning. When he was a logger, he sometimes began his day in the moonlight. No matter what came his way, he never gave up.

In 1976, Pop had three cardiac events in one weekend and was admitted to the Glens Falls Hospital where he stayed until the wedding day arrived for my brother, David. Against medical advice, my determined dad discharged himself and was present at the ceremony. Such was his fierce devotion to his family.

It was during that time that my dad began to read his Bible and watch Christian TV Programs. He knew that God had helped him in a big way, and he openly spoke about his faith in the Lord. Pop had to have an oxygen tank at home to help when he had chest pain and difficulty breathing, but he didn't let that hold him back. In the 1980's, he went back into logging and brought his oxygen tank right onto "Big John," his log skidder. If he ran into medical problems back in the woods, he would take a hit of 02 and "keep on trucking." That was my dad.

In 1986, Pop was diagnosed with prostate cancer, which had spread; and the doctors gave him only a short time to live. I remember him looking up at me from his hospital bed with those steel-grey determined eyes, and he said, "No way, Donald, I'm coming out of this bed." With the help of God, he came home. His journey through the next twelve years was filled with tremendous suffering as he endured chemotherapy, surgeries, and the awful pain from fourteen tumors. During Pop's dark valley, he just kept on going. His faith in the Lord was strong.

At a time when doctors were advising my dad to join a cancer support group, he was riding snowmobiles with my brothers. He had even installed a winch on his sled in case he got stuck off the trail!

In the summer months, he rode his 4-wheeler. Check out the photo on page 10.

Pop always had a great love for gardening, and in the spring of each year, he would plant corn, tomatoes, cucumbers, squash, strawberries, and even pumpkins for the grandkids. I still say that he grew the best corn on the planet! He built a vegetable stand on wheels and would tow it out front in the morning, complete with a coffee can for the proceeds. After his early morning harvest, he would rest in his hammock and periodically check out the coffee can. He and my mother would often use the earnings to go get a milkshake.

Pop also built a special four-wheel cart that allowed him to harvest his garden while sitting down. When the pain got too bad, he would lie down on the cart and keep right on harvesting the garden.

On November 17, 1998, Pop passed on to a better place. Without a doubt, he had the most impact of anyone on my life; and he will always be my "HERO." The following is a poem that God gave me just before my father's funeral.

A TRIBUTE TO POP

There was a new sound in Heaven
On that bright Eternal Day
The angels cried, "Lord, what is it?"
The Lord smiled and said," That's Ray.

"You see… he's got a chainsaw
That contraption will do us good
Cause we've been waiting forever
To get some decent firewood.

"And he will be fixing all sorts of things
Here in Glory Land
When all the others say it can't be done
I know Ray will say, 'it can.

"He's had a lifetime of experience
Providing for wife and family
And he helped all who crossed his path
And he did it all for Me.

"So now he's reached his heavenly home
And that really makes me glad
Cause he's a man after my own heart
For he gave all he had."

WELDING

CHAPTER 3

WEDDING BELLS

In January of 1972, I was a senior at Plattsburg State; and on the weekend, I was playing in a rock group at Dunham Bay Lodge in Lake George, NY.

I had been praying that I would meet a special young lady, and God answered my prayers. One day, I found out from the lead singer of our group that his wife was working with a single, 23-year-old RN at Glens Falls Hospital, Patty Stevens. Soon, arrangements were made for us to meet right at the lodge. We hit it off right away and discovered we had a lot in common. We both liked music, and we came from close knit families. We were both searching for God in our lives. Patty had a strong Catholic background and a precious faith. Just being with her brought out the best in me. That has never changed!

In May of 1972, I graduated from Plattsburg State with a BA degree in Sociology; and in June of that year, I proposed to Patty, the love of my life. She said, "yes!" In July, I received an expected draft notice, because I had been on a student deferment during my college years. I ultimately chose to enlist in the US Airforce on a delayed enlistment, with a report date of December 27, 1972.

Patty and I were married on October 7, 1972 and set out on a JOURNEY OF FAITH together.

After Basic Military Training and Air Force Tech School, in May of 1973, we were stationed at Plattsburg Airforce Base. It was located just sixty miles from the Canadian border. I was assigned to the base supply squadron, and it was there that I met Ralph Bess, who happened to be a Christian and worked in the neighboring office.

I can remember that I would frequently embarrass Ralph with my off-color humor and crude language, but he never gave up on me. He was just like that fella I had worked with at the amusement park three years earlier. He had God in his life, and that was obvious.

Ralph and his wife invited us to dinner one day, and soon we accepted an invitation to attend their church. I remember feeling self-conscience as we were the only white folks in an all-black Church. But you know what? The love and acceptance we felt from the people and the Presence of the Lord in that place was awesome. At the end of the service, everyone was holding hands down front, singing and praying to the Lord. We didn't make a commitment to the Lord that day; however, we were greatly moved by the love that we had experienced. We had begun our JOURNEY OF FAITH.

Ralph Bess completed his tour of duty, and he left the Airforce without fully knowing the impact that both he and his wife had made on our lives. One day,

I will give Ralph a huge hug in Heaven for his incredible witness to us!

Chapter 4

MY SPIRITUAL HERITAGE

"Owen, would you ask the blessing?" These were the words of my dad, speaking to Grandpa White on Thanksgiving Day, 1972. There were eleven of us gathered together in my parents' dining room on that special day. Patty and I were newlyweds, and this was her first Thanksgiving with our family. I will never forget that prayer, because it ended up being a song. In a burst of pure joy, Grandpa White exuberantly began to sing the Doxology and was immediately joined by Grandma White and then the rest of us.

"Praise God from whom all blessings flow
Praise Him all creatures here below
Praise Him above ye heavenly host
Praise Father, Son, and Holy Ghost. Amen"

I had never heard it sung like that before, with such passion and spontaneity. It was like the angels had showed up for Thanksgiving dinner! Maybe they had! By the time we sang, "Amen," I remember that tears were streaming down Patty's face.

Reverend Owen Jacob White and his wife, Lena, were the Patriarch and Matriarch of our family. I had always been in awe of my grandfather, who was always present on special occasions. He was a soft-spoken, yet powerful man of few words; yet, when he spoke, he had a lot to say. Grandma White was a very outgoing lady who had an incredible sense of humor and an infectious laugh. After hearing a funny story, she often would exclaim, “That's a corker,” and soon we all would be joining in with her laughter.

Grandpa White was an Ordained Minister with the Pentecostal Holiness Association, and he pastored churches in Bakers Mills, Comstock, and later in Warrensburg, NY, in the late forties and fifties. His wife, Lena, also shared with the preaching; and over the years, she filled several notebooks with beautiful sermons given to her by the Lord.

Grandpa once told the story of a time when everyone was seeking God at their church. The presence of the Lord became so strong that the church building literally shook. On another occasion, we heard the story of the time when a prisoner had escaped from the Comstock State Prison, which was a short distance from their home. Grandma had a vision from the Lord in which she saw exactly where the prisoner was hiding. She proceeded to call the State Troopers who then found the fellow right where she had seen him in the vision. I always knew that Grandpa and Grandma truly walked with God, and they had a profound impact upon our lives.

Grandpa White had always been a hard-working man who started out delivering milk in Fort Edward, NY in 1926. Two years later, he went to work on the Wait farm in Fort Ann, NY.

My mother recalled many happy memories there with her brother, Jake… swinging on a rope in the barn, playing with their four cats, and even sneaking some of Great-grandma White's homemade candy. I probably wasn't supposed to mention that!

In 1930, Grandpa and his family bought a house in Kingsbury, and he went to work at Union Bag Paper Company in Hudson Falls. He worked there for 19 years until he was called into the ministry in 1949 at the age of fifty-three. He sold his home to my parents and moved to a parsonage in Bakers Mills where he pastored his first church.

In the mid 1950's, he also pastored for a while in Warrensburg and then bought a small farm in Fort Ann. He also worked for a time in a local cheese factory. I can still remember being excited over the lunchpail Grandpa would bring filled with squeaky yellow curd cheese! Finally, in the early 1960's, Grandpa retired and bought a house in Comstock, NY.

In 1981, Grandma White went to be with her Lord at the age of 83. I remember at her funeral, Grandpa said, "Darling, I'll see you in the morning." He had his anchor in Christ.

Seven years later, Grandpa White was in the Glens Falls Hospital on a ventilator and in a coma. He had suffered a cardiac arrest. I took his hand in mine and expressed my gratitude to him and Grandma for the wonderful example they were to us all. As I quoted the 23rd Psalm, he squeezed my hand. He had heard every word. I purposed in my heart that I would carry on his torch, and I wrote the following poem in honor of his life.

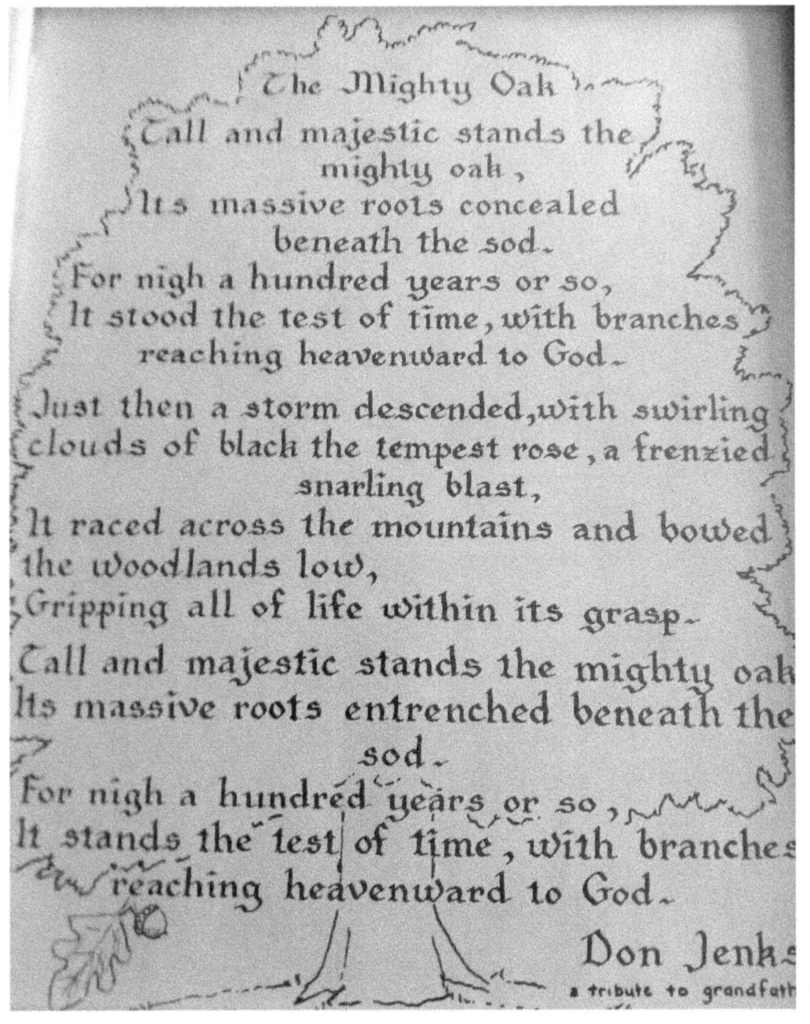

The Mighty Oak

Tall and majestic stands the
mighty oak,
Its massive roots concealed
beneath the sod.
For nigh a hundred years or so,
It stood the test of time, with branches
reaching heavenward to God.

Just then a storm descended, with swirling
clouds of black the tempest rose, a frenzied
snarling blast,
It raced across the mountains and bowed
the woodlands low,
Gripping all of life within its grasp.

Tall and majestic stands the mighty oak
Its massive roots entrenched beneath the
sod.
For nigh a hundred years or so,
It stands the test of time, with branches
reaching heavenward to God.

Don Jenks
a tribute to grandfath

CHAPTER 5

NEW BEGINNINGS

It was a beautiful evening in the summer of 1974. Patty and I were stargazing with Kim and Jim, our new friends from the Plattsburg Air Force Base. The sky was awesome, as was the warm summer breeze on the hill behind our tiny home. Suddenly Patty felt an urgency to check on Julie, our beautiful 13-month-old baby girl. What started out as a wonderful evening, in an instant, became a nightmare. Something was very wrong with our precious daughter. She had begun choking and was stiff all over. Patty, who was an RN, quickly assessed that Julie was in the middle of a fever convulsion. In a flash, we scooped up Julie in our arms and raced to the car.

The trip to the hospital seemed to take forever as Patty fought to keep Julie's airway clear as she began to vomit, and her cries were becoming weaker with each passing moment. “Dear God,” I prayed, “Please save my baby girl's life. I will serve you for the rest of my life!” Little did I know that God would hold me to that promise.

I found out that night how fast our Chevy Vega would go! With my heart in my throat, we ran into the Emergency Room at Champlain Valley Hospital in Plattsburg. The medical staff quickly began to suction

Julie's lungs. For the first time in my life, I felt truly helpless. I didn't want my baby girl to die. We needed God's help - big time! We continued to pray.

Our prayers were soon answered as Julie began to respond to treatment. “Da-Da,” she said through the oxygen mask. It is not possible to put into words the relief and gratitude that flooded our hearts. We had our daughter back! Julie had a very high fever that was caused by the Roseola Virus, and she was placed on medication. Soon, the crisis had passed, and a sense of normalcy returned to the Jenks’ household.

Unfortunately, I soon forgot the promise I had made to God and was back doing my own thing at the Air Base. I had forgotten about God, but He hadn’t forgotten about me. One day, I decided to go home for lunch; and I found Patty watching a Christian TV program. Normally, I would have made fun of the “religious fanatics,” but this time, I somehow felt different inside. The preacher on TV seemed to be talking right to me. He proceeded to describe my situation as if he knew me. “Young man,” he said, “You've been playing games with God, and He wants you to give your heart to Him right now.” I will never forget what he said next! “You are in a small ranch house on a hill, and you can see one tree from the road.” I began to tremble all over, because I was living in a Bungalow on a hill behind a motel. There was only one tree in front of our house that could be seen from the road!

There was no way that a preacher in North Carolina could possibly describe where I live. "God is REAL, and He KNOWS my address." In that moment, I suddenly remembered the promise I had made to God. Quietly, I knelt in my living room. No church choir… no stained glass windows… "Jesus, please forgive me of my sins and come into my heart." And you know what? He did. Patty had made a commitment to the Lord the previous day. That was over 51 years ago We have been serving Him ever since. Our daughter is now a wife and mother. God used a near tragedy to bring us to Him.

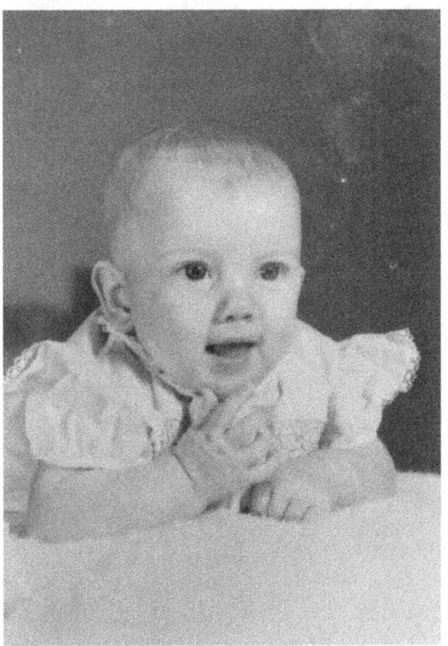

"For God so loved the world that He gave His only begotten Son, that whoever believes in Him should not perish but have everlasting life." John 3:16

CHAPTER 6

TESTIMONY

A short time after Patty and I accepted the Lord, God gave me the following song that expresses the change we experienced in our lives.

VERSE 1
Emptiness was all I found
Sun came up and the sun went down
Loneliness burning in my soul
Seemed like this was all I'd ever know
Just another face in the crowd
Quiet soul in a world so loud
All I wanted was life to end
Then one day, I met a Friend

INTERLUDE
There was a Man who lived long ago
Who just like me had an aching soul
He called to me from Calvary
He sent His love to set my soul free

CHORUS
The sweet love of Jesus saved my soul
The power of God has made me whole
Now I walk down that narrow way
Throughout eternity, I'll sing God's praise [repeat chorus]

VERSE 2

Sunshine burst on a cloudy day
A broken man had learned to pray
Now there rings a song in my heart
Now my soul sings Jesus
how great Thou art.

"Therefore, if anyone *is* in Christ, *he is* a new creation; old things have passed away; behold, all things have become new." 2 Corinthians 5:17

CHAPTER 7

THE TAPE RECORDER – 1976

A better tape recorder... that's what I need! Frustrated with the tiny cassette recorder I had, which by the way sounded like much like a squawk box, I asked God if I could somehow get a better one that would produce a more quality sound. I had begun writing Gospel songs and had fixed up a room in our tiny apartment for the purpose of recording. I didn't have any extra money at the time as my Airforce paycheck was very modest, yet I believed that God would answer my prayer.

Music has always been a very important part of my life, When I was four or five years old, I can remember being fascinated with my dad's old guitar that had a Hawaiian picture on it. The instrument only had three strings, but man, I played those three strings for all I was worth. When I was twelve, in the summer of 1963, I saved up my allowance and bought my first guitar from the Montgomery Ward Catalog for $16.95. I still can remember literally standing by the side of the road, waiting for my dad to get home, with my new guitar. It came complete with a chord book and a 45 RPM instructional record.

My friend, George Wilson, had just purchased his first guitar from the Sears and Roebuck Catalog. for $13.95, and he was just as excited as I was to learn how to play. There were no music teachers in Kingsbury; therefore, we had to teach ourselves. Before long, we had figured out how to play the basic chords, and we were having a great time. As time passed, our musical skills were developing quite well; and we began figuring out how to play Peter, Paul, and Mary songs such as “Blowin’ in the Wind,” “500 Miles,” “Stewball,” etc. We actually formed a folk group with help from my little brother, David.

Now, you have to understand that my brother was about four and a half years younger than George and me, and his voice hadn’t changed yet. This was great, because he could sing Mary Traver's part while George and I handled Peter and Paul's parts on the songs. We got so we could harmonize pretty well and actually had a chance to sing in public at the Kingsbury Parish Hall. I can remember being embarrassed to my toes, not because we sounded bad, but because my glasses fell off midperformance. Oh, well. It was during those years that I developed a fingerpicking style that would greatly enhance my Christian songwriting.

During this time, my brother, David, George, and I were attending the Kingsbury Baptist Church; and we were becoming very close to our new pastor, Reverend Patterson. He took a genuine interest in us and in our music. In fact, he let us borrow a reel to reel tape recorder to do our very first recording. It was an exciting time, although we did have a few harrowing moments when we thought we had broken the tape recorder. George's face turned beet red, and he put his fist clean through the wall. His poor mother decided to hang a picture over the devastation. I always did think the picture looked a bit unnatural, being so close to the floor and all!

Back to the original point… I was now 25 years old and was very excited about the songs God was giving me. I needed a quality tape recorder. A short time after my prayer, I noticed an advertisement on the Air Base, a Sony reel to reel tape recorder for $35.00. I remember thinking this must be a misprint. A recorder costs more than that! Especially a Sony! l quickly called the number and later met with a Seargent on the Air Base. The recorder was in excellent shape for just $35.

The Seargent, a total stranger, then said that he would wait for the money and let me take the recorder home. My intent was to borrow the money from a friend until payday. On the way home, I stopped at the local post office and was totally amazed! In the mail, I had received a refund check from the New York Telephone Company for $35 and change. I then raced home and excitedly shared this with Patty: “Here's my new tape recorder, and here's the money to pay for it.” God's timing was perfect! He had answered my prayer and was teaching me a valuable lesson about his faithfulness and provision.

“And my God shall supply all your need according to His riches in glory by Christ Jesus.” Philippians 4:19

CHAPTER 8

THE MOVE

It was December of 1977. It had been really difficult finding work after completing my tour of duty with the Air Force; however, I finally managed to find part-time work at Sears and Roebuck in the Auditing Department and also a second job in the Maintenance Department at Eden Park Nursing Home in Glens Falls, NY. Patty was also working part time at the nursing home as an RN.

Our daughter, Julie, was now four years old; and our daughter, JoEllen Marie, the precious new addition to our clan, was just ten months old. Years later, JoEllen would question why we gave her the name JoEllen. Please forgive my flashback. You see, in the third grade, I had a crush on a girl named, you guessed it, JoEllen. I always was taken with that name! But back to the story…

In my heart, I knew that God had a special plan for my life that would take me beyond the broom that I was now pushing and the humungous hall that stretched out before me. I had been praying off and on all day that I could somehow get a better job. After having cleaned several rooms, I knocked on the Social Work Assistant's door. Her room was next on my things to do list. She opened the door and seeing that she was meeting with a gentleman, I proceeded to ask when might be a good time to clean her office. I was told a convenient time to return, and I went about my business without another thought.

As I later found out, the man in the Social Work Office was a consultant who worked with all of the Eden Park Nursing Homes throughout New York State. After I had popped my head in the office just for a moment, the Social Work Assistant mentioned to the consultant that I had a BA degree in Sociology and was pushing a broom. That was the beginning of a miracle in answer to prayer. Within a short time, I was called into the Director's office, and I was informed that there was a Social Work Assistant opening at Eden Park Nursing Home in Cobleskill, NY. The Director also mentioned that there were also nursing positions available at that facility, and he was willing to put in a good word for Patty and me. God had answered my prayers in an awesome way!

I ultimately interviewed for the position and was hired. Patty was also hired as a nurse. This was to begin a new chapter in our lives.

Our next challenge was to find housing. I remember driving to Cobleskill in the middle of the winter in search of a place to rent. The weather was pretty bad, with lots of snow and ice. Patty suggested that we go to the nearest Assembly of God Church to make inquiry about housing. We had been attending Gospel Lighthouse Church in Hudson Falls, and it seemed like a good plan to get some help from fellow Christians.

Soon we found ourselves in the office of Reverend Wayne Hampton, Pastor of Calvary Assembly of God Church in Cobleskill. We were immediately impressed by his friendly manner and willingness to help us. We explained that we were new to the area and needed housing for our family of four.

As it turned out, Dwight Edwards, a deacon at the church, and his wife, Sue, had just purchased a house and had a mobile home for rent, a few miles out of town in Argusville, NY. Reverend Hampton made a quick call, and to our amazement, he dropped everything he was doing and drove us out to meet Dwight and Sue Edwards. It so happened that they were just about our age, and like us, they had two young children. Soon, arrangements were made for us to rent the mobile home, and on New Years Eve 1977, we began a new adventure in our JOURNEY OF FAITH.

Pastor Hampton soon discovered that I played the guitar, and after we had been attending Calvary Assembly for several months, he encouraged me to lead worship on Wednesday nights. With my heart pounding, I began a ministry that would be an important part of my life for years to come.

CHAPTER 9

THE MIRACLE

Man, it's cold in here, I thought, as my breath produced a white puff in the bedroom. The date was January 1978, and our family had settled into our mobile home on a country road in Argusville, NY. It was winter, and we were certainly experiencing the challenges of a blustery cold one. *Oh no*, I thought, *we must have run out of fuel*! My heart sank. With all of the expenses involved in moving, our funds were depleted. I had a few days until pay day, and filling the fuel tank was next on my list.

My first thought was to get my wife and two young children to a warm place. I made my way over to Gladys Edwards' home. She just happened to be the mother of Dwight Edwards, our new landlord from our church, whom we were renting from.

I then returned to our trailer and started praying about what to do. I remembered the promise in Philippians 4:19 which says, "And my God shall supply all your need according to His riches in glory by Christ Jesus." Our money had run out; however, our God had not. As I waited in prayer, I heard clearly in my mind, *Order the fuel*. It definitely wasn't me, because it didn't make any sense. When you have no money, you can't order fuel. The instruction had come in loud and clear, *Okay, Lord, here we go*!

I called the fuel company and placed the order. What happened a short time later was quite amazing. As I looked out of the window, I saw the mailman coming down the road followed by the fuel truck. As the fuel was being delivered into our tank, I went to the mailbox. In the mail, was a letter from my mom and dad along with a check with a note that said, “Use this for fuel.” They were not aware of our immediate need for fuel. I had made that check out to the fuel company, and God made sure it was covered! Once again, God had worked things out to meet our needs.

.

CHAPTER 10

THE CROSSROADS

It was February 1979, and I was looking for a better job. I recently had interviewed for an Employment Counselor position at the Schoharie ARC, which was a sheltered workshop for intellectually challenged adults; however, as I hadn't heard back from that agency, I was going ahead with another interview with the Schoharie County Mental Health Clinic, which was across the street. The mental health clinic offered a higher salary and better benefits; however, I had felt very good about the interview at the ARC. I was not sure about what direction to go in and had been seeking the Lord for guidance concerning this situation.

The Lord answered my prayer in a very unique way. What happened at the mental health interview was absolutely amazing. The day of the interview had come, and I found myself sitting across from the executive director getting ready for what I thought would be a standard interview. The Director looked at me and said three words: “Didn't you hear?”

I replied, “hear what”? The director explained that he had received a call from the ARC and that they had already decided to hire me. That was the end of the interview, and God had opened just the right door. You see, six months later, our son, James Alan Jenks, was born with developmental disabilities; and as I was working for the ARC, I had become aware of programs that eventually would help our son. You can completely trust the Lord, because He knows what is best for our lives!

"I know your works. See, I have set before you an open door, and no one can shut it; for you have a little strength, have kept My word, and have not denied My name." Revelation 3:8

.

CHAPTER 11

EIGHTEEN BELOW ZERO

In 1979, our family moved to a two-story house in Fultanham, NY. Patty was expecting our third child, and the two-bedroom trailer was no longer big enough for our growing clan. On August 3rd of that year, James Alan Jenks was born; and although we didn't have a lot of money, we certainly felt very rich. God had blessed us with a son! A few months later in December, with Christmas rapidly approaching, I had decided take on a second job to supplement our income.

One event stands out in my memory as though it happened yesterday. It was nearly midnight as I crossed the Jamesway parking lot in Cobleskill on my way home at the end of my shift. I was really tired and looked forward to getting home to my wife and three kids. It was incredibly cold outside… one of those nights where I was sure my breath could freeze solid and fall on the ground like a snowball.

Soon, I was rolling down Route 145 in my 1976 Plymouth Wagon, heading out of town into the country. The headlights cut like a glistening knife down the frozen highway. Suddenly, I was aware that the engine was beginning to hesitate. *Oh, no! Not here, not now!* Soon the telltale temperature gauge began to climb, and my heart began to sink. The engine died, and I rolled to a stop on the deserted road. “Oh, God,” I prayed, “please help me.” I thought about the thermometer dipping to 18 below, and I was ten or eleven miles from home. There was not one house in sight.

Now, at this point, I had been a Christian for a few years; and I knew one thing for sure. You can trust God. Don’t get me wrong. I was still scared! Sometimes life has a way of getting pretty intense.

What happened next was truly amazing. Within approximately one minute of my prayer, I saw the headlights of an approaching vehicle, a pickup truck that looked familiar to me. It went by slowly and then came to a stop. The driver turned around and pulled up behind me.

It was my friend Warren, running one hour late for his 11 PM - 7 AM maintenance job in Cobleskill. Warren was running late, but God was right on time. Warren had an extra gallon of antifreeze in his truck, and he poured it into the radiator. My car engine roared to life, and I was on my way home. The Bible tells us that God will never leave us or forsake us. He can be trusted!

CHAPTER 12

THE PEACH TREE

It was the summer of 1982, and our young family was living in a rented country house in the tiny Hamlet of Fultonham, NY. It was an exciting time as the kids were ages 2-9 years old, and there was never a dull moment… like the day we discovered our girls' newly rescued pet, Benji the crayfish, swimming around in our vaporizer.

I loved my job at the Schoharie County ARC Workshop - Toe Path Industries where I worked as a rehab counselor and had the joy of assisting individuals with disabilities to develop such job skills as packaging, collating, assembling, machine operation, janitorial, and food service... I will always remember the day when I went with Maynard, age 57, all around the building showing off his very first paycheck. He was so proud!

Patty and I were also excited about being a part of our church family at Calvary Assembly of God in Cobleskill, NY, where we both taught Sunday School. Concerning memories, I still remember the day when I found one of our Junior Boys industriously disassembling part of the table where we were all sitting. I'll never know where he got the screwdriver from. Well, after threatening him with the terror of going up into the adult worship service, the little cherub straightened up.

Then there was the memory of one of Patty's students who was three years old. When questioned by her mom about what she learned in Sunday School, she answered, “Noah, Mommy.”

Her mom then asked her who told Noah to build the ark? She replied, “Patty Jenks did.” Patty had done a great job in narrating the story and in a loud dramatic voice said, “Noah, build me an ark.” Even though we didn't have much money, we were enjoying our walk with Jesus; and we were about to learn an important lesson in our JOURNEY OF FAITH.

Times were hard for us financially in those days, and on one particular occasion, we were in a tough spot. It was two days until payday, and we had run out of food… no food in the house and no money to make a trip to the store. Now I knew from the Bible that God had promised to meet our every need; however, I couldn't help but feel my spirit sagging. It was pretty scarry, but God was about to show us how creative He is in meeting the needs of His children.

Patty noticed from our front porch something quite amazing. The gnarled, old, peach tree in our front yard was filled with ripe peaches! Neither myself nor Patty had seen any fruit on that tree until that moment, and trust me, if there had been any peaches on that tree, I already would have been eating them. Patty quickly gathered a harvest of golden peaches, and within a short while, she made some scrumptious peach pies. We lived on dessert until payday. That following year, that tree did not produce any fruit. We had experienced a miracle! God knew exactly when we would need the peaches, and He met our need!

CHAPTER 13

PATH THROUGH THE DEER

Our family always looked forward to the Sunday evening services at Calvary Assembly of God in Cobleskill, NY. Pastor Hampton and his wife always made everyone feel special, and there was something very precious about the happy songs of praise, the smiling faces of our church family, and the times of prayer and Bible study we experienced there. As I was leading worship, it was important that we arrive a little early so I could set up the music. As a result, we were traveling the speed limit-PLUS, shall we say five miles per hour? (Of course, you have never done that!)

So, we were sailing down Route 145, when suddenly, there was a herd of deer racing across the highway, right in front of our front grill. There was absolutely no opening in sight, and I had no time to put on the brakes. "Dear Jesus," we cried as the car raced towards certain disaster. The next thing I remember is that there were deer bounding towards my driver's door, and on the other side of the car, leaping just beyond the passenger's door. Everything seemed like it was happening in slow motion, much like horses on a carousel.

The car and our precious family passed through the herd of deer unharmed that night. I had read in the

Bible about the parting of the Red Sea, and we experienced that same protection of the Lord firsthand.

CHAPTER 14

PITSTOP COFFEE HOUSE

"Out, out, out." These were the words of Pat Case, the unconventional owner of the Pitstop Coffee House, who was bringing the evening to a close. There was no doubt it was time to go home. Pat and his wife, Judy, ran a storefront outreach to street people in Gloversville, NY where they would have Christian music groups come in each week and also provide much needed clothing and food items to the folks at the Coffee Shop. Pat was a "no nonsense" follower of Christ who was passionate about reaching street people with the Gospel Message, and in fact, he banned "church people" from attending his events for fear that they would scare away those attending the coffee house.

The sound man at the Pitstop was Ed Perrone who was responsible for telling Patty and me about the outreach. We first met Ed at the Vineyard Coffee House in Cobleskill, which was an outreach of our Church. Ed was the sound man for Sky Wing, a Christian rock group, that was ministering at the Vineyard. Ed invited Patty and I to come minister at the Pitstop and after our first appearance made an incredible offer to us. He said that he had a recording studio and would like to record us. It was the summer of 1985 when we entered the JC Power and Light Studio and recorded our first music tape, *Jesus Made the Difference.* Ed subsequently recorded three more music albums for us, the last one being in 2002. It was an exciting time as we had the privilege of ministering at the Pitstop for several years.

During our time of ministry there, we witnessed the transformation of many lives. One young lady, who at first would not make eye contact with us, eventually was beaming with the love of Christ. On one occasion, an older man, who was broken from being an alcoholic for several years, poured a bottle of whiskey down the drain as he accepted Jesus as Lord and Savior. Because of Pat and Judy Case, and Ed Perrone, we were encouraged to continue developing our music ministry, which has been a part of our lives ever since that time. I am looking forward to giving those folks a big hug in Heaven for the part they played in encouraging us on our JOURNEY OF FAITH.

CHAPTER 15

THE DUMP TRUCK

"Dear Jesus, please give me traveling mercies," I prayed as I backed out of my driveway. I remember thinking that it was unusual for me to say that prayer unless I was going on a big trip. But you know what, it's better to be safe than sorry. It was a bright, beautiful day; and the commute to the Warren-Washington ARC was uneventful. Within 20 minutes, I pulled into the parking lot and made my way to the office.

Soon after I was seated at my desk, Sharon, a co-worker, came in and hurried over to me. She looked absolutely blown way. Her complexion was ashen, and with a quivering voice she exclaimed, "Don, did you see what almost happened to you?"

Quickly, I rehearsed my uneventful drive to work and answered, "No, why do you ask?"

"Don, there was a dump truck behind you when you stopped to turn into the parking lot. He never saw your turn signal, and at the last second, he jammed on his brakes. There is no way he could have missed you!"

Not only had I not experienced an inevitable crash, but I didn't even hear the squealing tires. I then looked at Sharon and told her that I had prayed for God's protection as I drove to work that day. She responded, “Well, the Man upstairs certainly is watching out for you.”

Psalm 121:7-8 says: “The Lord shall preserve you from all evil; He shall preserve your soul. The Lord shall preserve your going out and your coming in from this time forth, and even forevermore.” Praise the Lord for His protection!

CHAPTER 16

SUE'S PRAYER

The year was 1988, and our family was living in Adamsville, NY, near my hometown; and we and had settled into a comfortable routine. Our girls were attending Hartford Central School, and our son was enrolled in a nearby Special Education program. Patty was working at the Gospel Lighthouse Learning Center, and I was enjoying my job at Saratoga ARC, working as an Intake Coordinator and Vocational Evaluator.

What was really awesome was that we were living near my parents, and we were enjoying weekly visits with them.

After being away for several years, we had moved back into the area in 1985. We were enjoying reconnecting with family and friends. It certainly was a special time. I assumed that this situation would continue for years to come.

However, my assumption was wrong. You see, the year 1985 was significant as Sue and Dwight Edwards, our friends from Calvary Assembly in Cobleskill, NY, were now pastoring Readburn Assembly of God Church in Hancock, NY. As the year 1988 rolled around, they informed us of a job opportunity that I was qualified for at Delaware County Mental Health Clinic near them.

The employment opportunity seemed very appealing; however, after careful consideration, I decided not to apply for the job as it would involve uprooting my family once again from my hometown area. Leaving the comfort zone and the familiar is not an easy thing to do.

Well, like I said, I had decided not to take the job and was planning to let Sue and Dwight know about my decision to turn down the opportunity.

I was on my way to work when it happened… it's really hard to put into words exactly what happened. I suddenly felt the incredible Presence of the Lord, to the point where I began to tremble. In my mind, I heard the words, “You are to go.” There was no doubt, I was to go.

I immediately called Patty from work and told her what happened. I subsequently applied for the job and was hired by the Delaware County Mental Health Clinic in December of 1988.

We were on the road again! What I didn't know was that Sue Edwards had been led to pray for us to come to Readburn to lead worship. I also didn't know that I not only would become the worship leader there, but one day in 2006, I would become the pastor of Readburn Assembly of God Church.

God sees the big picture, and you can trust Him 100%! Proverbs 3:5-6 states: "Trust in the Lord with all your heart, And lean not on your own understanding, In all your ways acknowledge Him, And He shall direct your paths."

CHAPTER 17

GOD, MY REFUGE

In 1988, I began working at the Delaware County Mental Health Clinic as a case manager. People who received therapy at the clinic, sometimes were dealing with very difficult situations such as homelessness, no income, legal problems, etc., and they would be referred to my department to receive practical assistance in dealing with their pressing issues. Sometimes I would be called upon for crisis intervention, and the first person to hear about a problem was Sandy, our animated receptionist. She and I had a running joke that started one day when she said, "Don, we've got a crisis."

And I responded, "I'm not Don. I'm his twin brother, Pedro." From then on, she called me Pedro and would encourage me to "get a grip."

On one occasion, the receptionist informed me that BOCES had called, and one of my clients was extremely upset and was asking to speak with me. Now this was very concerning as the young man in question had reportedly been involved with organized crime in the past. Immediately, I jumped into my county car, a tiny Plymouth Horizon, and set out on the ten mile ride to BOCES. Upon arrival, I quickly noticed that the young man was pacing back and forth on a basketball court outside and was not responding to a teacher's attempts to calm him down. The young man recognized me when I called out to him, and he agreed to get in the car with me. I had decided to take him to the clinic due to his high level of agitation.

While en route to the clinic, the young man stated that he had a knife on him and he felt like using it. He then began to hyperventilate and exclaimed that he saw "blood running." At that moment, with my heart pounding, I jammed the accelerator pedal to the floor and began to quietly pray in the Spirit. Within a minute, he stopped hyperventilating and became completely quiet. We arrived at the clinic without further incident, and due to the potentially dangerous situation, the Walton Police Department was called. The officer proceeded to disarm the young man who did in fact have a knife on him. The young man agreed to go to the hospital to receive support and treatment.

9-21-99

Hi Pedro!

Just a note to say we miss you alot! Things here are as crazy as ever!

How is the new job going? And Patti, how is she?

I'm sending a few pictures of your party. It was great fun! but we all ate to much. (whats new?)

Let us hear from you.

Love,

Sandi

LITHOBID®
(Lithium Carbonate, USP)
Slow-Release Tablets, 300 mg

"God is our refuge and strength, a very present help in trouble." Psalm 46:1

CHAPTER 18

THE ANGEL

In 1999, Patty and I accepted a temporary assignment in Hackettstown, NJ where Sue and Dwight Edwards were then pastoring. We were serving on a worship team at Calvary Assembly of God Church.

In order to support ourselves, I had taken a job at the Center for Educational Advancement as a vocational evaluator, and Patty was providing in-home daycare a short distance from where I worked.

It was around 4:30 PM when I picked up Patty from work, and we began the 30-mile commute on a busy New Jersey highway that led back to our apartment in Hackettstown. It had been a very busy day for both of us, and we looked forward to having a nice dinner and a relaxing evening.

Suddenly, the car engine began to hesitate and then completely died as the car rolled to a stop… the tires crunching on the edge of the road. *Oh, no! What are we going to do?* I thought. We didn't have cellphones, and we were sitting partially off the road on a dangerous curve.

"Dear Lord," we prayed, "please help us." Within just a few minutes of that prayer, someone pulled up right behind us and out stepped a mountain of a man with a big beard. Without a word, he proceeded to step out into the middle of the road; and with both arms extended, he stopped the traffic!

He then approached our vehicle and instructed me to put my shifter in neutral. He then pushed our car completely off the road and handed me a cell phone saying, "Call whoever you need to." I called Dwight Edwards, and soon arrangements were made for a tow truck and for a ride home for us. I handed the phone back to the man and thanked him, and he left without a word. Just a man? Or was it an angel? Thank you, Jesus, for your help in times of need.

In 2001, as planned, we returned to Walton, NY and Readburn Assembly of God Church.

CHAPTER 19

OMAR

"What must I do to be saved?" This was the question posed to us as we pulled into Omar's driveway. This elderly gentleman had just attended the morning service at Readburn AG Church and had been greatly moved by the message. Patty and I then spoke about the free gift of Salvation and led him in the sinners' prayer. Omar became a "Born Again Christian" that day and became a faithful attender of our church. Patty and I had agreed to pick him up for service and provide transportation as needed. It's really quite amazing how the Lord brought Omar into our lives. Omar called the parsonage one day stating that he wanted to attend our church service. We later learned that he actually thought he was calling the Walton Assembly of God Church but was very happy to attend the Readburn Church where he sensed acceptance by the church members and the Presence of the Lord.

Omar's only income when we met him was donations received for taking care of some 40 cats and 20 dogs. Shortly after our meeting him, he retired from caring for animals and rented an old schoolhouse in the country. There was one major problem with this situation. The building had no heat, and it was winter! Fortunately, one of our church members was a furnace repairman, and soon arrangements were made to install a hot air furnace. As Omar was a senior citizen and now had no income, I connected him with Social Services and the assistant director went out of his way to track down necessary paperwork to obtain a social security card and Social Security benefits.

Omar was a very interesting man. He was an immigrant from Cuba and shared with us that in the past he was the drummer on the *I Love Lucy* show, and he also worked as an extra in Hollywood movies. The waitresses, one day at the local diner in Walton, NY, were shocked as a stretch limo from MGM Studios pulled up. As it turns out, Olivia de Havilland, a friend of Omar, had decided to visit him and treat him to lunch. One of our church members actually saw Omar performing in Dezi Arnaz's band on an *I Love Lucy* show rerun. Omar had a deep love for God, and at one prayer meeting, he had a vision of Jesus walking up and down the aisles of our church. He even described Jesus' sandals in detail.

Omar is with the Lord now, and one sweet day, we will have a reunion in Heaven with this special man that God brought into our lives.

CHAPTER 20

THE CALLING

Patty and I accepted the Lord Jesus into our hearts in 1975, and that event changed our lives. During the years that followed, we became involved in several Assembly of God churches working in the ministry areas of Children's Sunday School, Worship Team, and Puppet Ministry. Additionally, we developed our own music ministry that featured original Christian/Gospel songs; and we had the opportunity to record five music albums. For several years, I had been taking Berean correspondence courses; however, I had never been led to apply for ministerial credentials. I was content to be a singer/songwriter, worship leader, board member, and Sunday School teacher; however, God had other plans in mind.

In 2005, we were attending the Readburn Gospel Assembly of God Church, and as our pastor had left, we had an interim pastor, Ismael Berrios, doing pulpit supply. It was during that time that Ismael began calling me, "Pastor."

"No way!" was my response. I remembered the words of my former pastor, Dwight Edwards, who said, "If you're not called to be a pastor, it will eat you up." Man, I didn't want that at all! Over the years, as a board member, I had experienced firsthand the challenges that ministry can bring to a pastor, such as people upset by the color of carpet, time and day established for a ministry, length of service, etc. During those times of conflict, I was very glad that I wasn't the pastor.

Nevertheless, Ismael persisted in calling me, "Pastor," and as a result, I began to pray about God's perfect will for my life. After a while, instead of responding with "No way," I soon found myself just smiling. Then it happened... the Holy Spirit spoke to my heart that I was to complete the required coursework for ministerial credentials in preparation for pastoral ministry. Now, you've got to understand that this did not at all seem practical. After all, at this point, I was 55 years old, an age that AARP considers you to be a senior citizen. None the less, the call of God had come, and I set out to complete the required courses.

In 2006, I completed the courses; and after interviewing with the Presbyter of the South the Central Section of the Assemblies of God, I was granted credentials. As Readburn Assembly of God Church did not as yet have a fulltime pastor, I applied for the position. Even though I had been an active member of the church for 16 years and was a board member, it would not be an easy process to become a candidate for the position. As the church membership dwindled to less than twenty, it was considered a revitalization work, therefore Patty and I were required to participate in an eight-hour interview.

During that time, no stone was left unturned as our life was scrutinized by two interviewers. Yes, I even had to confess my speeding ticket in 1985. Our kids were late for choir practice, and we became even later as the flashing red light appeared in my rear view mirror just as we were pulling into the church parking lot. It was embarrassing as Patty and I were scheduled to do a special song in the morning service at the Gospel Lighthouse Church. We did successfully complete the interview, and ultimately, I was voted in as pastor in 2006.

God was faithful to give me a pastor's heart, and He equipped Patty and me to successfully revitalize the work at Readburn Church. We pastored there from 2006-2014, and finally at the age of 63, I was led to return to my hometown where we began attending Granville Assembly of God. The Lord enabled us to purchase a home in Comstock, NY, and I secured a job at Rutland Mental Health Services as an employment coordinator. From 2014-2017, Patty and I were happy to be a part of the worship team at Granville AG and also the Lighthouse outreach to children.

We thought that would be the full extent of our ministry. Wrong! Then it happened again! In the Summer of 2017, as I was driving by Faith Chapel Assembly of God (Whitehall, NY) on my way to work, I began to feel like I was supposed to apply for a pastoral position there. The previous pastor had left the church, and the Lord was tapping me on the shoulder. As I reflect on the events of my life, I am reminded that my Grandfather, Rev. Owen J. White, had been called into the ministry at the age of 53 and that I had made a promise to him as he was on a ventilator at the Glens falls Hospital that "I would carry on the torch." God held me to that promise.

Maybe you feel that you are not able to do much in God's Kingdom, or perhaps you feel the best years of your life are past. Keep your heart open! You just might be a candidate for another divine assignment. If you are not yet a Christian, please know that God loves you very much; and if you will invite him into your heart and life, you will begin a Great Adventure!

Readburn Assembly Of God Welcomes New Pastor

On Wednesday, November 15, the membership of Readburn Assembly of God Church, elected Rev. Donald Jenks to the position of Pastor.

Don and his wife Patty have been active members of the church for several years and are now looking forward to leading this Assembly in their new post.

On Sunday, January 7, at 11:00 a.m. an Installation service will be conducted by Rev. Larry Frank, Executive Assistant, NY District Assemblies of God. The Rev. Dwight Edwards, former Pastor of Readburn A/G will take part in the Installation ceremony. A dinner will follow the service.

Church Address: Readburn Gospel Assembly of God, P.O. Box 688, Hancock, N.Y. 13783. Church Phone: 607-637--4832, Parsonage 607-865-6773 (after Dec. 4)

CHAPTER 21

NEVER ALONE

The really awesome thing about being a follower of Christ is that you are never alone. As a young man, before I came to a saving knowledge of the Lord Jesus Christ, I wrote the following poem that described how I felt inside:

ALONE

I walked the black night through
With the wind and the pale moonbeams in a midnight pact
The road too was submerged in gloom
And with fleeting shadows at my back
The crunch of gravel underfoot
Appalled stillness to tears

Since Patty and I came to the Lord on our JOURNEY OF FAITH, we have had the joy and privilege of being a part of the family of God. When we were living away from our hometown and family and friends, our church family was there for us offering friendship, support, and encouragement during our mountaintop and valley experiences… and that has been continuing to this very day!

At Faith Chapel, where we currently pastor, we have been blessed time and time again as we dealt with my cancer diagnosis, Patty's open heart surgery in 2019, and flooding of our home two times. One amazing source of support has been our small group that meets every week. It's there that all who come are able to share their victories as well as their heartaches and receive much needed prayer and support.

Not only has our church family been there for us, our Lord has been there through all the challenges of our life, answering our prayers and providing for our every need. In the Bible, we have an awesome promise: "I will never leave you nor forsake you." Hebrews 13:5b

This promise is true. We have lived it! On December 27, 2024, Patty had a heart attack. At the Glens Falls Hospital ER an ECG revealed that she had a 75% blockage of her heart, which then set in motion a cardiac team that completed an emergency heart catheterization. After being told the scary news, Patty said, "I need to pray," and that she did. Meanwhile, I had called members of our church and asked them to pray. Patty came through the procedure with flying colors. It was what the surgeon said afterwards that was truly amazing. He said that as the surgery progressed, when they got in there, they discovered it was not nearly as critical as they originally believed. The heart blockage was already dissolving! We know that God, the Great Physician, had intervened! When you walk with Christ, you are never alone.

The following is a poem written by my sister-in-law when she was going through a difficult medical challenge during chemotherapy:

YOU ARE NOT ALONE

A poem written by Carol A. Jenks

You do not walk alone upon the rode of life,
You do not need to fret whenever there is strife,
For Jesus walks beside you upon your lonely trail,
He will never leave you and He can never fail.

But you must ask His guidance, though He is always near,
And you must seek His presence and you need never fear.
For Jesus always answers the knock on Heaven's door,
And once you let Him in, He's there for evermore.

Then you must yield to His great power,
And let Him lead you hour by hour.
A mighty joy will fill your days,
While others tell you of His wondrous ways.

Study His Word and meditate,
About His love and see how great,
Your life can be when you will choose,
Your life, in Christ, you do lose.

Later, when on Heaven's shore,
You meet the King whom you adore,
And see your loved ones there to greet,
And throw your treasures at His feet.

CHAPTER 22

SO, WHAT ABOUT YOU?

In this little book we have shared some highlights from our story. What is your story? Has it been clear sailing or a bumpy ride? I suspect that you have endured many storms in your life. For the Bible says: "Yet man is born to trouble, as the sparks fly upward." Job 5:7

When I was a little boy, I would watch my dad grinding a part out in the garage on his bench grinder. I would be fascinated by the sparks that flew off the little machine. Lo and behold, they flew upward! Well just as certainly as that happens, we all face trouble in our life. Fortunately, Jesus tells us in John 16:33, "These things I have spoken to you, that in Me you may have peace. In the world you will have tribulation; but be of good cheer, I have overcome the world."

So, what is your story? Perhaps you are an atheist and don't believe in God. That means you have put all of your hope in the few short years you're here on earth. There is real HOPE, Eternal Hope; His name is Jesus. He is just a prayer away. Maybe you once believed in God but now you are not so sure. Let me assure you that His existence doesn't depend on our level of faith. He does exist, and as we put our faith and trust in Him and what He accomplished on the cross, we discover His existence.

Maybe you have fallen away. If so, there is forgiveness and restoration. His name is Jesus. Maybe you've never asked Jesus into your heart and life. It's never too late.

John 3:16 declares that "God so loved the world that He gave His only begotten Son, that whoever believes in Him should not perish but have everlasting life."

What your life has been does not have to be what it will be. God is in the restoration business. If you want a brand-new start on a Great Adventure, just say this prayer:

Dear Lord Jesus, please forgive me for all of my sins and cleanse me from all unrighteousness. I ask you, Jesus, to come into my heart and become Lord of my life. In Jesus' Name, Amen.

If you prayed this prayer and meant it with all of your heart, you are now "Born Again," born of the Spirit. You have now begun the Great Adventure… a JOURNEY OF FAITH.

We would love to hear from you if you have made the decision to follow Christ. We can be reached at djpj49@outlook.com.

In my JOURNEY OF FAITH, I learned to take time out to listen to the voice of God, I pray that you, too, will learn to hear His voice.

www.ingramcontent.com/pod-product-compliance
Lightning Source LLC
LaVergne TN
LVHW020653100826
845148LV00012B/2469

* 9 7 9 8 2 3 4 0 7 2 5 7 3 *